C++ Better Explained

The intuitive beginner's guide

Preface

It was December 2014 just before the Christmas holiday period and here I was sitting on the train home almost having tears coming out of my eyes because I had just lost my undergraduate electrical engineering job. At the time, it was a big blow to me but it was a blessing in disguise because, in the end, I didn't want to be an electrical engineer. I wasn't a fan of ladder logic programming as compared to C++ and Java programming, because it was like going back to caveman times using it.

In that same year of 2014, I had written and published my first book called "How to win at Mathematics", which unexpectedly became a best seller on Amazon in the field of mathematics study and teaching in the USA and Australia for 18 months straight. After witnessing the high-level failure rate of C++ being taught at my university and as well as other universities, I decided that I wanted to write the C++ book that I wish existed when I first started learning the language back in 2009.

So after a drunken night out on New Year's Eve out in Melbourne which I stayed up all night, I came home surprisingly unhung over, slept for a few hours then woke up to begin writing the very first edition of C++ Better Explained.

Fast forward to 2020, and yet here I am still making an impact of having the absolute pleasure to teach C++ to thousands of people worldwide with the help of all the free content I have published, the book that is in your hands right now to the students who I have taught in a one on one setting.

The reason why I have kept doing this for so long is because of all the positive feedback from all my students, who have achieved amazing results from consuming my content and all the amazing projects they have worked on which has left me astonished.

Relax you are in good hands. Just stick by me and I will show you the ropes.

Sahil Bora, Melbourne, Australia. January 2020

Acknowledgments

To everyone who has supported my ideas and bring them to life, I couldn't have done it without your support. Special thanks to my business mentor Sylvester Nkongho who helped me with all the copywriting and marketing of this book. Without you, I couldn't have done this. To my team of editors and designers who have designed a beautiful cover for this book and have taken the time to edit my writing, I can't thank you enough. Also to you, for giving me a chance to serve you in teaching the C++ programming language.

Testimonials of C++ Better Explained

"I had never done any programming before and then suddenly I had to take a class in C++ programming, and I was struggling. Sahil was able to break down and explain to me everything in plain simple English. I was then able to confidently pass the class" – Patrick Saad

"I was failing the C++ programming assessments because my lecturer was terrible at teaching the material. I then discovered the C++ Better Explained book and I was able to understand the concepts in less than an hour and teach it to my struggling peers. Get this book if you are struggling to learn C++" – Mohammad Alsarraf

"I would say for a beginner guide for C++, this is the book. I wanted to learn because I was engaged with a project that required this programming. I was lucky to get this book. It has a good guide for a beginner and I learnt a lot from it. Thanks" – Sharon Gielen

"No confusing, direct, to the point and with good examples to see, understand and remember. Good job, please continue to write books." – M.L

"Your stuff is very digestible. I like how you explain this stuff, it's very down to earth and reable. Kudos." – Calvin Pulliam

"Very well organized and spells out C++ very well. Well worth the investment. Highly recommend! – Scott Cleveland

Sahil great book, well set out. The diagrams are what sets your book apart. Different learning styles require different approaches. Lines and lines of code mean nothing to someone who is a visual learner. Your diagrams make understanding much easier for visual learners. It is the initial first steps where someone either gives up or continues. – Michael Heenan

I was really delighted when I saw this book which simplified the C++ language and which was something that I really needed. I always perceived learning C++ as very taunting and challenging, but I really liked how Sahil put things into pieces, goes straight to the point, at least allow the reader to dig deeper. The way I put the book was very appealing in that sense. – Boris Houenou

I have experience in many other languages. Without it I'm not sure I'd be able to get through this text at the half way point and beyond. I do like the direct approach and feel this will be a good reference for beginning programmers. – Michael McFarren

Contents

Introduction

Computer programming can be a difficult thing to learn, especially when you have no programming experience at all. There are hundreds of thousands of resources online to learn computer programming, as well as thousands of books published today. It's worse when you are in university and are forced to take a programming class, where the concepts are not explained well enough and you are forced to write code for a test and you have no idea what you are doing.

A lot of people hate computer programming because most of the time, it is taught in a dull and boring manner, which is fair enough to say. I can understand where they are coming from. I remember taking an elective in high school that taught Visual Basic and the teacher didn't even know how to code at all, so he just gave us a textbook on Visual Basic and made us program the examples in the book. At the start I had no clue what I was doing, but I slowly started figuring it out.

I started gaining more of an interest in computer programming and wanted to learn another language. I was interested in video game development. After some research, I found that C++ was the language of choice for that area. My first C++ resource I purchased was "Ivor Horton's Beginning Visual C++ 2008" back in 2009, when I was 15 years old. It was a massive book with over 1000 pages. I started coding the examples in the book but I had no idea what I was doing.

From memory, it took me about three months to understand a simple program containing integers, strings and decisions. Over time, I started to understand the concepts of C++ object orientated programming to a point where I started taking on exciting programming projects in C++.

Fast forward to 2014, where I was in my second year of engineering and a core subject we had to complete was programming in C++. The class was taught in a dull and boring way, with people either distracted or falling asleep. It showed that nobody had understood anything the lecturer was teaching because 90% of the class failed the mid semester practical coding test.

I was tutoring friends in person and on Skype during the semester with assignments and programming concepts because most people had never learnt computer programming before. When you are forced to learn C++, a complex object orientated programming language, it can be a nightmare. I was more than happy to share my developed understanding of the language to my friends to help them pass the class.

This book is dedicated to effectively learning and understanding C++, in which beginners can completely understand in a fun visual and intuitive way. 95% of programming books today are just huge textbooks with thousands of pages with code samples and a brief explanation of concepts. This book is something I wish existed when I was a complete beginner programmer as I struggled for months trying to code the simplest things such as functions, variables and operators in C++ which I had no clue about.

I hope when you go through the book, the concepts start to click in your mind and save you hours of frustration. Enjoy!

A brief history of C++

The development of the C++ programming language was started in 1979 by Bjarne Stroustrup. It was originally named C with classes as the language is a major extension of the C programming language. Stroustrup stated that the purpose of C++ is to make writing good programs easier and more pleasant for the individual programmer.

As the language advanced, more developers started using C++ instead of C because of its support of being an object-orientated language with a high performance. Today's software developed in C++ includes the following examples:

- Adobe Systems
- Apple OS X
- Autodesk
- Facebook for several high performance and high reliability components
- FlightGear
- GCC
- Google Chrome
- Intel
- Microsoft Windows operating systems
- Mozilla Firefox
- Modern computer games and graphics engines
- Symbian OS
- ZeroC

The C++ language influenced several other modern programming languages such as Java, C# and Perl. If you can master the concepts of C++, then you will have no problem learning another object- orientated language like the ones I listed earlier.

Compilers

There are many compilers to program with C++. It's a matter of personal preference but in the code samples in this book will be from code running from Microsoft Visual Studio, as it my favourite integrated development environment.

Here is list of compilers that can be downloaded for free of use. There will be instructions online on how to setup each IDE but I will show you how to start a new C++ project in Visual Studio.

- Apple Xcode
- Bloodshed Dev C++ (Not recommended as it is very outdated)
- C++ Builder
- Cygwin GNU C++
- CodeWarrior
- Digital Mars C++
- Microsoft Visual Studio C++ express edition
- Oracle C++
- RAD Studio

Starting a new C++ project in Visual Studio

Step 1: Start Visual Studio by launching it from the shortcut from your desktop or by finding it in "all programs"

Step 2: Click "Create a new project"

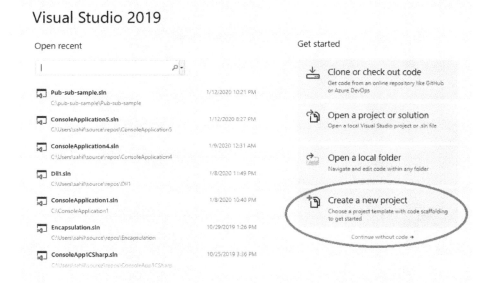

Step 3: Select Console App C++ and click next

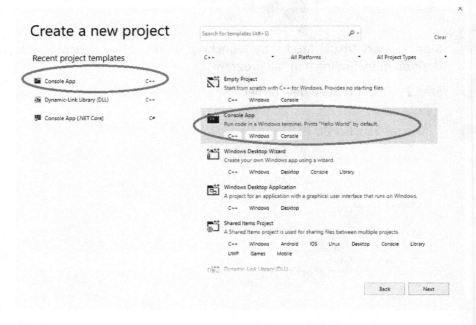

Create a new project

Search for templates (Alt+S) 🔍 ▾   Clear

C++ ▾   All Platforms ▾   All Project Types ▾

Recent project templates

📁 Console App   C++

🔳 Empty Project
Start from scratch with C++ for Windows. Provides no starting files.

C++   Windows   Console

📰 Dynamic-Link Library (DLL)   C++

🔲 Console App (.NET Core)   C#

Console App
Run code in a Windows terminal. Prints "Hello World" by default.

C++   Windows   Console

Windows Desktop Wizard
Create your own Windows app using a wizard.

C++   Windows   Desktop   Console   Library

Windows Desktop Application
A project for an application with a graphical user interface that runs on Windows.

C++   Windows   Desktop

Shared Items Project
A Shared Items project is used for sharing files between multiple projects.

C++   Windows   Android   IOS   Linux   Desktop   Console   Library
UWP   Games   Mobile

Dynamic-Link Library (DLL)

Back   Next

Step 4: Enter in a name for your project and then click create

Configure your new project

Console App   C++   Windows   Console

Project name

YourFirstProject

Location

C:\Users\sahil\source\repos   ▾   ...

Solution name ℹ️

YourFirstProject

☐ Place solution and project in the same directory

Back   Create

6

Step 5: You're now ready to start programming a C++ project

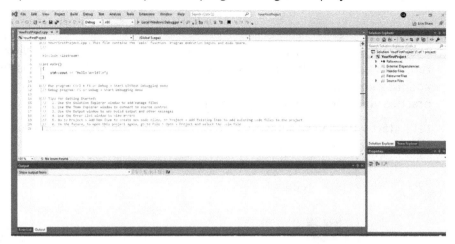

A simple C++ program

The best way to learn programming in any language is by coding and running example code. Programming is not something that can't be learnt and mastered by just watching. You have to put in the time by putting it into practice yourself and making plenty of mistakes to get the hang of it.

Let's start with a very simple C++ program. With the source code below, it has the fundamentals that every C++ program has

```
1   // My first C++ Program
2   #include <iostream>
3
4   using namespace std;
5
6   int main()
7   {
8       cout << "This is my first C++ program\n";
9
10      return 0;
11  }
```

```
C:\Windows\system32\cmd.exe
This is my first C++ program
Press any key to continue . . .
```

Let us now examine the code of our first program so we understand what is going on.

Line 1: // My first C++ Program

Two slash signs show that it is a comment inserted by the programmer. They do not affect the code because they are ignored by the compiler. Comments are important in because programmers use them to explain what is happening in the code or observations.

Another way to comment code is by code blocks with:

/*

This is my first C++ program

*/

Line 2: #include <iostream>

Lines starting with a hash tag sign (#) indicate that we are including what we call a header file. Without this, we cannot perform standard input and output operations, such as writing the output of "This is my first C++ program" on the screen.

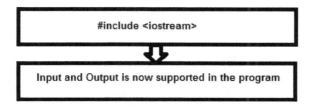

Line 4: using namespace std;

This is an important line of code because this links up the standard C++ library. When code becomes more and more complex, this line of code is also designed to differentiate similar functions, classes and variables with the same name in different libraries. In other words, with the help of "using namespace std", it stops the compiler from mixing up code with similar names and identities.

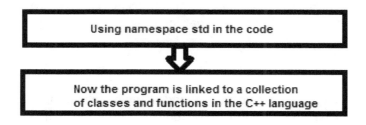

Line 6: int main()

Without this line of code, the program will not start. It is just like trying to start a car without a battery. The execution of all C++ programs begin with the "int main()" function in the code. It doesn't matter where is it located in the code, without it, the program will not run.

Line 7: {

The open bracket indicates the start of the main's function definition. It is the main area where you implement code of what you want the program to achieve

Line 8: cout << "This is my first C++ program\n";

In this line of code, we are asking to display "This is my first C++ program" onto the screen with the help of "cout << ". This is the body of the program. You can see that there is a "\n" in the line of code. This means I am asking for a new line after the text has been displayed.

Line 10: return 0;

This line terminates the "int main()" function and causes it to return the value of 0. For the majority of operating systems such as Windows, Mac OS X, a return value of 0 ensures that the program is terminating normally.

Line 11: }

This closed bracket indicates the end of the main's function definition. After you have written the code in the body, you close it with a "}"

Below is a visual diagram of the sample code implementation in simple block form and the fundamentals of a C++ program. If you can understand this diagram, then you can understand a basic C++ program.

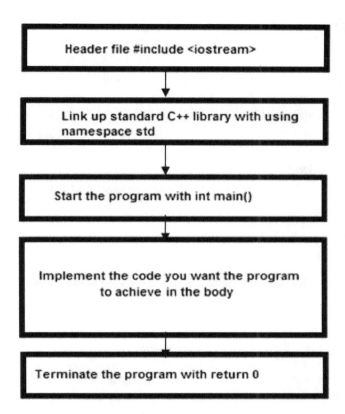

Header file #include <iostream>

Link up standard C++ library with using namespace std

Start the program with int main()

Implement the code you want the program to achieve in the body

Terminate the program with return 0

Syntax errors

Syntax errors happen when you try to compile your code but it will not run. The compiler does its best to make sense of what code you have typed when it tries to run it. They cannot be ignored because if they are not fixed, the program will not run. Finding where you made mistakes gets easier with experience and practice. The advantage with Visual Studio is that in the error list, it will tell you where the problem is and how to correct it.

	5 Errors	2 Warnings	0 Messages
	Description		
1	error C2065: 'ghgfhf' : undeclared identifier		
2	error C2143: syntax error : missing ';' before 'if'		
3	error C2143: syntax error : missing ';' before 'if'		
7	IntelliSense: expected a ';'		
6	IntelliSense: identifier "ghgfhf" is undefined		

What are the types of syntax errors?

Missing a semi colon - When you are declaring variables and have lines of code in the body, the line must end with a semi colon.

```
// Integer variables
int i, j

// Set variables
i = 5
j = 6;
```

	Description	
1	error C2146: syntax error : missing ';' before identifier 'i'	
2	error C2146: syntax error : missing ';' before identifier 'j'	

Undeclared identifier - This comes up when the compiler does not recognise a variable name because you either have not created it or you mistyped it.

```
int k;
cout << u;
```

⊗ 1   error C2065: 'u' : undeclared identifier
📄⊗ 2   IntelliSense: identifier "u" is undefined

Variables and data types

What is a variable?

A variable is something which is stored in the random access memory on your computer. It will contain a known or unknown value of information. In simple English, a variable stores data. Variables are one of the most useful things in programming because it's what allows you to control your character in a video game or pay your bills via online banking.

How do we declare variables with identifiers?

An identifier is a name given to a variable that can contain letters, underscore characters and digits. Punctuation marks, special character symbols such as @#$% and spaces cannot be included in naming an identifier. A rule with naming identifiers is that it cannot begin with a digit.

Examples of identifiers include the following:

string name;

int number1;

float number2;

char _character;

bool happen;

What the heck are "string", "int", "float", "char" and "bool" doing next to the identifier name?

To declare a variable identifier, we must give it a certain variable type. These are called keywords and C++ uses several keywords to identify operations and data descriptions. The most common C++ keywords used in creating variables are

bool - Stands for boolean. The value of bool is either 1 or 0 because it is a true or false value.

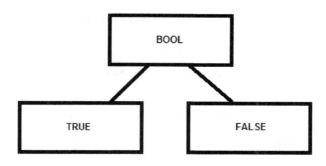

char - Char stands for Character. It will store a single number, a single letter or a single special character. Chars cannot be used for mathematical calculations. An example of declaring a char value is:

char two = '$';

char three = '9';

When you are declaring a char value and it is a single letter or single special character, you must equal it with a single quotation mark at the start and end with '$' followed with a semi colon to end the declaration.

int - The most common C++ keyword used in the language. Stands for integer which holds integer quantities from -32,767 to 32,767.

double - Handy for calculations in C++ which restrict the variable to two decimal places. The advantage of double is that supports calculations with decimals as int does not support it.

float - Floating point variable. It's similar very to a double but can store less values than a double.

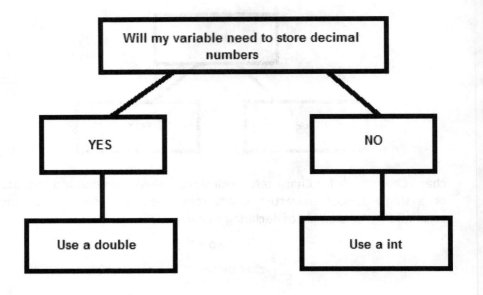

string - A string is a useful C++ keyword as it can store a series of characters that can be used again in another part of a C++ program. If you are going to be using strings, you will need to declare the string header file #include <string> up the top of the code with #include <iostream>

Here is a visual description of a string. The rectangular black box represents a string and the red text "I am learning C++" is the series of characters stored in the rectangular box.

"I am learning C++"

An example of actually declaring a string is

string name = "I am learning C++";

Putting all these things together into a program.

Here's an example of a program using the C++ keywords we have just learnt to calculate the value of a hypotenuse of a triangle. In Mathematics, finding

16

the hypotenuse of a triangle is done with the help the of Pythagoras theorem formula.

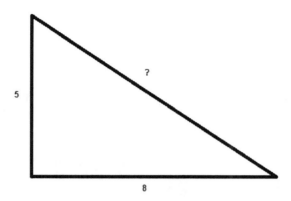

```cpp
1  /* Pythagorus theorem program to
2      Calculate the hypotenuse of a triangle
3
4      Written By Sahil Bora
5  */
6  #include <iostream>
7  #include <math.h>
8  #include <string>
9
10  using namespace std;
11
12  int main()
13  {
14      // Variable identifier declarations
15      string title = "Pythagoras theorem";
16
17      // Triangle values
18      double a = 8;
19      double b = 5;
20
21      // Result of the triangles
22      double result;
23
24      // Calculate the value of the hypotenuse
25      // sqrt is part of the <math.h> header library
26      result = sqrt(a*a + b*b);
27
28      // The main program output
29      // "\n" means newline
30      cout << title << "\n";
31      cout << "The hypotenuse is\n" << result;
32
33      return 0;
34  }
```

```
C:\Windows\system32\cmd.exe

Pythagoras theorem
The hypotenuse is
9.43398Press any key to continue . . .
```

So let us run through Pythagoras theorem code output. At the start of the program, the string "title" is being displayed at the start just as I instructed. Then the program calculates the value of the hypotenuse. As soon as that is done, the program outputs "The hypotenuse is" then the calculated value "9.43398".

Table reference of common C++ Variables

Type	Keyword	Variable Range
Boolean	bool	1 or 0
Character	char	-127 to 127 or 0 to 255
Integer	Int	-214783648 to 2147483647
Double floating point	double	
Floating point	Float	

Operators

Operators in computer programming can instruct the program to perform mathematical or logical operations. With the help of logical operators, we can use them to operate variables we have defined.

Arithmetic Operators

Operator	Meaning
+	Addition
-	Subtraction
*	Multiplication
/	Division
%	Modulus
++	Increment
--	Decrement

What is the % operator?

This is called the modulus, which is represented by a percentage symbol. It stands for modulus division which finds the remainder of a calculated division in a program. Here's an example.

```
1  /* Modulus division simulation
2
3      Written By Sahil Bora
4  */
5  #include <iostream>
6  #include <math.h>
7
8  using namespace std;
9
10 int main()
11 {
12     // Result variable of the modulus division
13     int x;
14
15     x = 11 % 3;
16
17     // Display the remainder value from the modulus division
18     cout << x;
19
20     return 0;
21 }
22
```

Result of the modulus division of 11 divided by 3

What is increment and decrement?

The operators ++ and -- are the increment and decrement operators. The simplest way to explain them is that they are shortcuts for addition and subtraction in programming.

For example

x = x + 1;

is actually the same as x++

and x = x - 1;

is the same as --x;

Does it matter where I put the ++ and -- when I am implementing increment or decrement?

21

++x is known as a pre increment

x++ is known as a post increment

In this simple example, there is no difference where you place the ++ or -- in your code. But if you are dealing with a large expression, it can become an important difference. Remember to always test your code when you are implementing increment or decrement operations as the compiler cannot pick up logical errors.

```
1   /* Increment and Decrement example
2
3       Written By Sahil Bora
4   */
5   #include <iostream>
6   #include <math.h>
7
8   using namespace std;
9
10  int main()
11  {
12      // Variables for pre and post increment example
13      int x;
14      int y;
15
16      x = 5;
17      y = 7;
18
19      // Pre increment value of x
20      ++x;
21
22      // Post increment value y
23      y++;
24
25      cout << "x value pre increment value" << "\n" << x << "\n";
26      cout << "y value post increment value" << "\n" << y << "\n";
27
28      return 0;
29  }
```

In this sample program of pre and post increment, the values of x and y have been incremented by one with the x value starting with 5 and the y value starting with 7. With the results shown below, it is showing the end result operation of pre and post increment.

```
C:\Windows\system32\cmd.exe
x value pre increment value
6
y value post increment value
8
Press any key to continue . . .
```

Logical operators

In C++, logical operators deal with true and false statements acting together. In logic, this can be AND, OR, NOT. The symbols used for these operations are in the following table.

Logical operators	Meaning
&&	AND
||	OR
!	NOT

```
1  /* Logical operators in action example
2
3      Written By Sahil Bora
4  */
5  #include <iostream>
6
7  using namespace std;
8
9  int main()
10 {
11     // Values used for logical operators
12     bool value1;
13     bool value2;
14
15     // Set values to true and false
16     value1 = true;
17     value2 = false;
18
19     // AND Operation
20     if(value1 && value2)
21         // This will not be displayed because this logical operator
22         // will not work
23         cout << "This won't work\n";
24
25     // NOT AND Operation
26     if(!(value1 && value2))
27         cout << "!(value1 && value2) works\n";
28
29     // OR Operation
30     if(value1 || value2)
31         cout << "value1 || value2 is true\n";
32
33     return 0;
34 }
```

```
C:\Windows\system32\cmd.exe

!(value1 && value2) works
value1 || value2 is true
Press any key to continue . . .
```

Let's look at what is going on with the code. This may be tricky to understand at first but let's go through line by line to see what's happening. Don't worry about the "if" keyword just yet. They will be taught in the chapter "program control statements".

Line 11 and 12: We are just declaring two boolean values to be used for the logical operations. We cannot use int or double because they deal with numbers.

Line 16 and 17: The two boolean values are now being initialised with a value. Value1 is being set to true and Value2 is set to false.

Lines 19 - 23: The first logical operation being used is an AND operation. As you can see in the simulation, cout << "This won't work\n"; is not being displayed in the simulation. The reason why it is not showing is because value1 && value 2 are not both true and false. One is different from the other, thus line 23 will not be outputted in the simulation.

AND Operation diagram

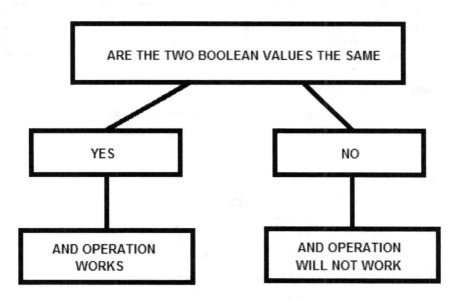

Lines 25 - 27: This is very similar to lines 19 - 23 but if you look closely, there is a "!" before the expression (value1 && value2). "!" represents NOT, so since value1 and value2 are the not the same, it will display in the simulation "!(value1 && value2) works".

Lines 29 - 31: An OR operation being implemented here. This is the opposite of the AND operation. If value1 and value2 have different values, it will display "value1 || value2 is true" in the simulation.

OR Operation diagram

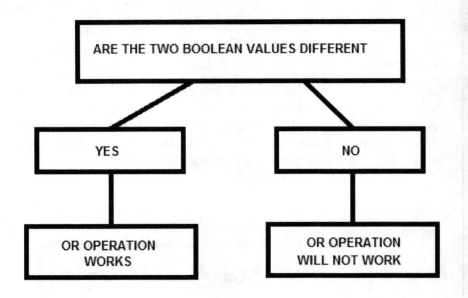

Relational operators

These operators deal with logic operations such as less than, equal or greater than. These are not as difficult as logical operators and can easily be mastered.

Operator	Meaning
>	Greater than
<	Less than
>=	Greater than or equal to
<=	Less than or equal to
==	Equal to
!=	Not equal to

```
1  /* Relational operators
2
3      Written By Sahil Bora
4   */
5  #include <iostream>
6
7  using namespace std;
8
9  int main()
10 {
11     // Integer variables
12     int i, j;
13
14     // Set variables
15     i = 5;
16     j = 6;
17
18     // Relational operators
19     if(i < j)
20         cout << "i is less than j\n";
21     if(i > j)
22         cout << "i is greater than j\n";
23     if(i != j)
24         cout << "i is not equal to j\n";
25     if(i == j)
26         cout << "i equal to j\n";
27     if(i >= j)
28         cout << "This wont work\n";
29     if(i <= j)
30         cout << "i is less than or equal to j\n";
31
32     return 0;
33 }
```

```
C:\Windows\system32\cmd.exe

i is less than j
i is not equal to j
i is less than or equal to j
Press any key to continue . . .
```

I am sure this is going to be easier to understand than logical operators. The value of i is 5 and value of j is set to 6. In the code, I am programming the computer to question the following

27

- Is i less than j

-Is i greater than l

-Is i not equal to j

-Is i equal to j

-Is i greater than or equal to j

-Is i less than or equal to j

The lines that are true would be displayed in the output simulation.

Basic input and output

In almost every single computer program today, there is basic input and output. From your smart phone, entering numbers and text on the keypad, pushing buttons on a video game controller to control a video game character and everywhere on Facebook, you can input comments and status updates.

In C++, basic input and output is used with "cout" and "cin". In the previous chapter, we have been using cout to display text and numbers. In this chapter, we will demonstrate the use of "cin" in programs.

So what is this keyword "cin"

The standard input when developing computer programs is the keyboard. When you are installing Microsoft Windows for the first time, you cannot use a mouse as the default input is the keyboard.

Here is an example program, asking the user what their age is and displaying it when it is entered:

```cpp
1  /* Enter in my age
2
3     Written By Sahil Bora
4  */
5  #include <iostream>
6
7  using namespace std;
8
9  int main()
10 {
11     // Store the age in this variable
12     int age;
13
14     // Ask the user what their age is
15     cout << "What is your age\n";
16
17     // The user will enter in their age
18     cin >> age;
19
20     // Display what the user entered in
21     cout << "You are " << age;
22     cout << "\n";
23
24     return 0;
25 }
```

```
What is your age
20
You are 20
Press any key to continue . . .
```

Program control statements

In programming, we can implement decisions in our code to execute a specific instruction. There are two main statements in C++ where this can be achieved. Selection statements with *if..else* and switch statements. Iteration statements are known as for loops, while loops and do loops.

Selection if else statement

The general form of a if else statement is

```
if (condition)
{
    statements;        // executed if condition true
}
else
{
    statements;        // executed if condition false
}
```

where if the result of the expression is true, the first statement is executed, otherwise the second statement is executed.

In this example, a simple *if else* statement is shown below, where if the user enters in a number greater or equal to 10, it will output "The number you have entered is greater than 10."- If the user entered in a number less than 10, it will show, "The number you have entered is less than 10. "

```
1   /* If else statements
2
3       Written By Sahil Bora
4    */
5   #include <iostream>
6
7   using namespace std;
8
9   int main()
10  {
11      // Variable to get a number from the user
12      int number;
13
14      cout << "Enter in a number ";
15
16      // Get the user to enter in a number
17      cin >> number;
18
19      // When the number is greater or equal to 10
20      if(number >= 10)
21          cout << "The number you have entered is greater than 10";
22
23      // When the number is less than 10
24      else
25          cout << "The number you have entered is less than 10";
26  }
```

Greater or equal to 10 output

```
Enter in a number 15
The number you have entered is greater than 10
```

Less than 10

```
Enter in a number 9
The number you have entered is less than 10
```

Nested if..else

A nested if else statement deals with a more complex control statement, but it can be easily understood visually with the diagram below.

32

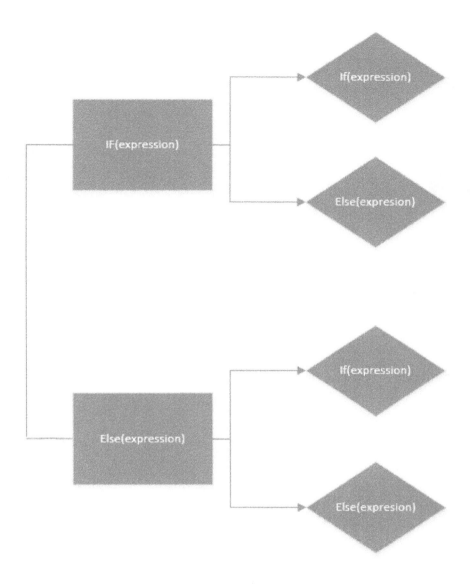

The nested *if..else* statement being applied here in the code below is a program where you enter in your age to find out what your risk getting into an accident by driving. If you are 21 or under, the program will check to see if you are either 18 or below. It will then show your risk. If your age is greater than 21, it will check to see if your age is equal or less than 23, and then display your risk.

```cpp
/* Nested if..else statement

    Written By Sahil Bora
*/
#include <iostream>

using namespace std;

int main()
{
    // Store the age input here
    int age;

    cout << "Enter in your age to find out what your risk of\n";
    cout << "driving a car is\n";

    // Enter in age
    cin >> age;

    // The age is less than or equal to 21
    if(age <= 21)
    {
        // Age is less than or equal to 18
        if(age<= 18)
        {
            cout <<"Very high risk";
        }
        else
        {
            cout << "High risk";
        }
    }

    else
    {
        if(age <= 23)
        {
            cout << "Medium Risk";
        }
        else
        {
            cout << "Low Risk";
        }
    }
}
```

```
Enter in your age to find out what your risk of
driving a car is
20
High riskPress any key to continue . . .
```

Multi way decisions if else statement

Multi way decisions are different from nested if..else statements because instead of creating another inner if..else statement, it just uses "else if" in the next line.

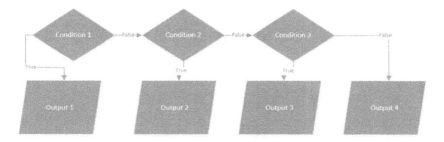

The sample multi way decision code is a program to calculate university grades by getting the user to enter in their final grade mark. When the user has entered in their grade, the multi way statement will compute the grade the user has achieved.

```
int main()
{
    // Store the mark entered in
    int mark;

    cout << "University grade calculator\n";
    cout << "Enter in your mark to see your grade\n";

    // Enter in the student mark
    cin >> mark;

    // The Multi way statement will then give the grade
    // To the screen
    if(mark >= 80)
    {
        cout << "High Distinction\n";
    }
    else if(mark >= 70)
    {
        cout << "Distinction\n";
    }
    else if(mark >= 60)
    {
        cout << "Credit\n";
    }
    else if(mark >= 50)
    {
        cout << "Pass\n";
    }
    else
    {
        cout << "Fail\n";
    }
}
```

Sample output of the university grade calculator

```
University grade calculator
Enter in your mark to see your grade
66
Credit
```

Switch statement

A switch statement works exactly like multi way decision statement but in C++, it is known to be more efficient than if else statements. The switch expression must evaluate to either a character or a constant integer value. Integer values with a specific range are not supported in switch statements.

When dealing with larger programs, switch statements have the advantage because the value of the expression is successively tested with a list of constants. Those constants are known as the "case" in the code. When a match is found in the switch statement, the specific line of code is executed in the program.

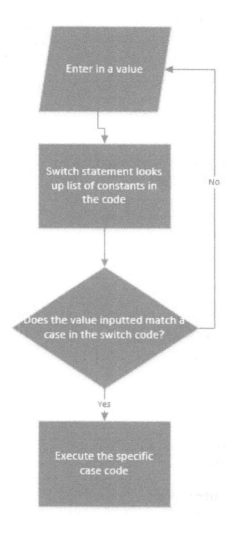

In the switch statement code sample is a program where the user enters in a number between 1 - 12. Once the number has been inputted, the program will then take the number inputted and match it to a case in the switch statement, and then display the month.

```cpp
/* Switch statement

  Written By Sahil Bora

 */

#include <iostream>
using namespace std;

int main()
{
        // The variable used to look up the month
        int month;

        cout << "Enter in a number between 1 - 12 and the month will\n";
        cout << "Show up\n";
        cin >> month;

        switch(month)
        {
        case 1:
                cout << "January";
                break;
        case 2:
                cout << "February";
                break;
        case 3:
                cout << "March";
                break;
        case 4:
                cout << "April";
                break;
        case 5:
                cout << "May";
                break;
        case 6:
                cout << "June";
                break;
        case 7:
                cout << "July";
                break;
```

```
        case 8:
                cout << "August";
                break;
        case 9:
                cout << "September";
                break;
        case 10:
                cout << "October";
                break;
        case 11:
                cout << "November";
                break;
        case 12:
                cout << "December";
                break;
        }
}
```

The for loop

A for loop is an iteration statement that has been designed in C++ to repeat a number of times. The loop repeats while the condition is true and the loop breaks when the condition is false. For loops can be useful for counter variables as they support setting variables at the start and increasing the value before the loop begins.

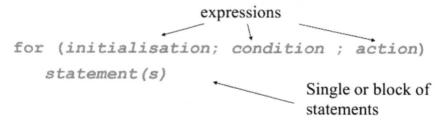

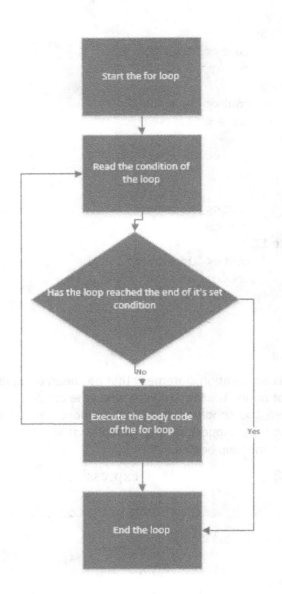

```
1  /* For loop code
2
3       Written By Sahil Bora
4    */
5  #include <iostream>
6
7  using namespace std;
8
9  int main()
10 {
11     // The i variable is the initial variable
12     for(int i = 0; i <= 3; i++)
13     {
14         cout << i << ", ";
15     }
16
17     cout << "GO\n";
18 }
19
```

The for loop code is a program that counts from zero to three, then outputs "GO" when the loop has completed. As you can see in the for loop, variables and program operators that we have previously learnt are being applied here.

While loop

The while loop just repeats code while the condition is true. When the condition is no longer true, the loop will stop running. The general form of a while loop is

while(condition)

{

        statement;

}

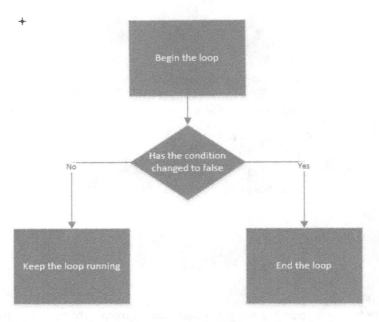

The while loop code below is a rewrite of the previous for loop program which would count from one to three then display "GO". Instead of using a for loop, we are using a while loop here.

```cpp
/* While loop code

    Written By Sahil Bora
    */
#include <iostream>

using namespace std;

int main()
{
    int j = 1;

    while(j <= 3)
    {
        cout << j << ", ";
        j++;
    }

    cout << "GO\n";
}
```

The do-while loop

The do while loop is similar to the while loop as it acts like a while loop but the condition is evaluated after the loop begins instead of before. The do while loop is always guaranteed to be executed at least once when it is used.

The general form of a do-while loop is:

```
do  {
    statements;
}  while (condition);
```

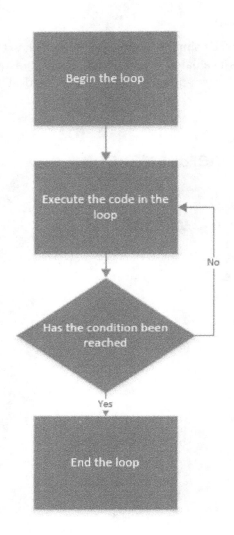

```
 1 ⊟/* Do while loop
 2  │
 3  │    Written By Sahil Bora
 4  │  */
 5  │  #include <iostream>
 6  │
 7  │  using namespace std;
 8  └
 9 ⊟int main()
10  │  {
11  │      int numberinput;
12  │
13  │      do
14  │      {
15  │          cout << "Enter in a number\n";
16  │          cout << "\nIf you enter the number 1, the program will end\n";
17  │
18  │          cin >> numberinput;
19  │
20  │      } while (numberinput != 1);
21  │      // Program will end if number 1 is inputted
22  └}
```

The do while sample code is a program where you type in a number and it will keep running until you type in the number 1. As you can see in the simulation output, since I have entered in one, the program has now shut down by displaying "Press any key to continue".

```
Enter in a number

If you enter the number 1, the program will end
50
Enter in a number

If you enter the number 1, the program will end
60
Enter in a number

If you enter the number 1, the program will end
95
Enter in a number

If you enter the number 1, the program will end
1
Press any key to continue . . .
```

Arrays

An array is a collection of elements of the same variable type that are placed in contiguous memory locations that can each be individually referenced. The way it can be individually referenced is by adding an index to the identifier.

Normally one dimensional arrays are more common because they are useful for holding characters and string variables.

The general form of declaring a **one dimensional array** is:

variable_type variable_name[size];

For example, an array containing five integer values of the variable type int could be represented visually as:

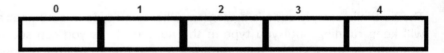

The sample code below will output the elements in the array

```
1  /* One Dimensional arrays
2        No values have been set in the array
3
4      Written By Sahil Bora
5   */
6  #include <iostream>
7
8  using namespace std;
9
10 int main()
11 {
12     int sample[5];
13
14     // Load the array
15     for(int i = 0; i < 5; i++)
16     {
17         cout << i << "\n";
18     }
19
20     return 0;
21 }
```

Output from the example code above

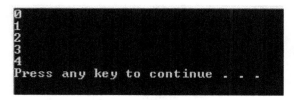

Setting and displaying array values

By default, regular arrays are left with no set values. The elements in an array can be set to specific values when it is declared with braces like the example below:

int sample[5] = {10, 20, 50, 100, 200};

0	1	2	3	4
10	20	50	100	200

The elements then can be outputted on the screen with the help of the for loop code. Firstly you must output the array variable name which we named "sample" then you must type in "[i]" after it so the for loop elements are displayed.

// Load the array

```
for(int i = 0; i < 5; i++)

{

            cout << sample[i] << "\n";

}
```

```
1  /* One Dimensional arrays
2       Values have been set in the array
3
4       Written By Sahil Bora
5  */
6  #include <iostream>
7
8  using namespace std;
9
10 int main()
11 {
12     int sample[5] = {10, 20, 50, 100, 200};
13
14     // Load the array
15     for(int i = 0; i < 5; i++)
16     {
17         cout << sample[i] << "\n";
18     }
19
20     return 0;
21 }
```

Output of the set array values

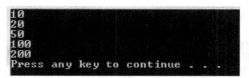

Two dimensional arrays

The simplest way to describe a two dimensional array is that it is list of one dimensional arrays which can be described as "array of arrays" in simple terms. The way two dimensional arrays are declared is:

int twoDimensional[3][5];

The visual way to see is declaration is with the diagram below

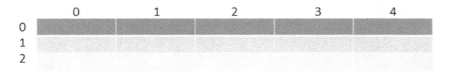

In the sample code below, a two dimensional array is loaded with the numbers 1 through to 15 and is indexed by "(i*5) + i+1;". When the code is running, the value of twoDimensional[0][0] will have the value of 1, twoDimensional[0][1] has the value 2 and so on.

Two dimensional arrays can be complex to understand at first but they can be useful for sorting data stored in arrays. Don't worry if you don't understand them now, come back later and try and to write own code of two dimensional arrays.

```cpp
1  /* Two Dimensional arrays
2
3     Written By Sahil Bora
4  */
5  #include <iostream>
6
7  using namespace std;
8
9  int main()
10 {
11     // Two Dimensional array declaration
12     int twoDimensional[3][5];
13
14     // Loop through the first array [3]
15     for(int i = 0; i < 3; i++)
16     {
17         // Loop through the second array [5]
18         for(int j = 0; i < 5; j++)
19         {
20             // Times the values of array i by 5
21             // Indexing the variable Two Dimensional
22             // requires two indexes
23             twoDimensional[i][j] = (i*5)+j+1;
24
25             // Display the values of the two dimensional arrays
26             cout << twoDimensional[i][j] << "\n";
27         }
28     }
29
30     return 0;
31 }
```

Pointers

One of the reasons why C++ is such a powerful language is because of the concept of pointers in the language. It is also one of the most difficult things to understand and can be misused in the code which can create problems further down the track.

What are pointers?

A pointer is an object that contains a memory address, which is often linked to the location of another object as a variable. There are two types of operators which pointers use which are * and &. To understand the concept of pointers, we first have to understand how variables in a program are stored. We know that variables are stored in the random access memory (RAM), in which the RAM consists of memory cells, a byte long in size that contains a unique address.

Using an analogy to break down and understand pointers, we are going to create an analogy of the RAM containing houses on a street, where each house is a memory cell. Now there must be a way for use to find the house we want. Well each house on the street has a different colour so this would be our variable name:

Int house_white;

Currently, house_white does not have a value stored so continuing on, we will give it a value of 50.

house_white = 50;

This will now store the value of 50 to the variable house_white, Remember that the variable house_white is now a unique number stored in the memory. If house_white was number 500 in the memory, we would know that the house is between houses 499 and 501 when we are searching for it.

The general form of declaring a pointer is

variable_type *variable_name;

The & operator of pointers

The "&" symbol is known as the address of an operator. This operator would return the memory address of its operand. Following on from the houses analogy, the & operator would allow us to find where the house is located on the street.

$$house\_red = \&house\_white$$

This line would store the address of house_red variable into the variable house_white. Suppose the address of house_white is 500.

$$house\_white = 50;$$

$$house\_blue = house\ white;$$

$$house\_red = \&house\_white;$$

So in the first line will store the value of 50 in house_white. In the second line will store the value of 50 in house blue but in the third line, it will store the address of the variable house white, which is 500 in this example into the house_red variable.

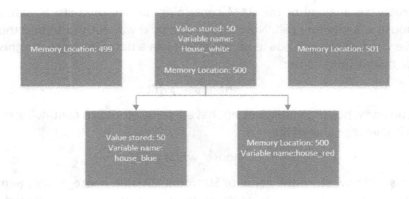

The * operator of pointers

The "*" symbol is known as the dereference operator. It basically takes a pointer to a value and then returns the value. It returns the value of the variable located at the address specified by its operand. Continuing on with the houses on the street analogy example, what if we wanted to know what the value stored at which house_red was pointing at. This is where the "*" is applied to find the value pointed by:

$$house\_search = *house\_red;$$

This will store the value of 50 in the house_search variable. Following our analogy, house_search will ask house_red what value it is storing. It will show to be 500. The variable house_search will then go the location of where the house is located, which is 500 and enquire what the value is stored in that house. That house, which is the value house_red, will show the value to be "50". So house_search will now know to store 50 in his search.

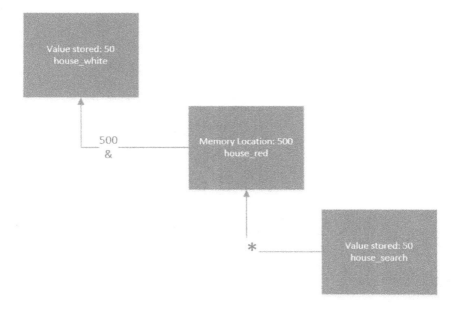

Below is some code that puts the operators of pointers into practice

```
1    /*
2    Pointer sample code
3    */
4
5    #include <iostream>
6
7    using namespace std;
8
9    int main()
10   {
11       // The house variables
12       int house_white;
13       int *house_red;
14       int house_search;
15       int house_blue;
16
17       // Assign the value of 50 to house_white
18       house_white = 50;
19
20       // Obtain address
21       house_red = &house_white;
22
23       // Obtain value at the address
24       house_search = *house_red;
25
26       // Output the value at the address
27       cout << "Address is " << house_red << "\n";
28
29       // Output the value of the address
30       cout << "Total is " << house_search << "\n";
31
32   }
33
```

```
Address is 00CBFBEC
Total is: 50
Press any key to continue . . .
```

Pointers and arrays

In C++ programming, there is a close relationship with pointers and arrays. Arrays work very similar like pointers and an array can always be changed to the pointer of the proper type. Here's an example of arrays and pointer being mixed together where the pointer is being increment in the code.

```
1  /* Pointers and arrays
2
3      Written By Sahil Bora
4  */
5  #include <iostream>
6
7  using namespace std;
8
9  int main()
10 {
11     // Array of number declaration
12     int arraynumbers[5];
13
14     // De reference operator of the pointer
15     int *p;
16
17     // Return the memory address
18     p = &arraynumbers[0]; *p = 10;
19
20     // Increment the pointers and set the values
21     p++; *p = 20;
22
23     p++; *p = 30;
24
25     p++; *p = 40;
26
27     p++; *p = 50;
28
29     // Loop through the array and display
30     // The array and pointer elements
31     for(int i = 0; i < 5; i++)
32     {
33         cout << arraynumbers[i] << ", ";
34     }
35
36     return 0;
37 }
```

Output of the pointer and array code

```
10, 20, 30, 40, 50, Press any key to continue . . .
```

Input and Output with files

The C++ Standard library can help perform tasks from inputting and outputting text and results to/from files. Previously, we have used the cin/cout keyword to input/output text in the program, but in this chapter we will cover input/output from files.

The main C++ keywords we normally use to perform input and output to three stream classes are:

- ofstream: write on files

- ifstream: read from files

- fstream: Reads both read and writes from/to files

Below is an example of the ofstream being applied in the code

```cpp
/* Writing to a textfile

   Written By Sahil Bora
*/
#include <iostream>
#include <fstream>
using namespace std;

int main()
{
    // Create and open the file to write to
    ofstream textfile("thefile.txt");

    if(textfile.is_open())
    {
        // Write the following to the text file
        textfile << "I am writing this to a text file\n";
        textfile << "This is another line\n";

        // When finished writing, close the text file
        textfile.close();
    }

    // If there is a problem with the text file
    // Display this message
    else
        cout << "Unable to open file";
    return 0;

}
```

Output of the sample code written to a text file

thefile - Notepad

File   Edit   Format   View   Help

```
I am writing this to a text file
This is another line
```

In this sample code, the "ifstream" keyword is being applied here to read what is in the textfile

```cpp
/* Reading a textfile

   Written By Sahil Bora
*/
#include <iostream>
#include <fstream>
#include <string>

using namespace std;

int main()
{
    // Use a string to read each line in the textfile
    string line;

    // Open the existing textfile
    ifstream textfile("thefile.txt");

    if(textfile.is_open())
    {
        // Read each line of the textfile
        while(getline(textfile, line))
        {
            cout << line << "\n";
        }

        // Close the textfile when the reading is complete
        textfile.close();
    }

    // If the file does not exist, display the error message
    else
        cout << "Unable to read file";

    return 0;
}
```

Output of the "Ifstream" being applied in the code

```
I am writing this to a text file
This is another line
Press any key to continue . . .
```

Open a file

When you are working with non existing or existing files, the first thing you must do is open a file. Without opening the file, the input/output of files will not work and the C++ standard library will not be able to help do its job of opening/reading files.

With the previous code examples, in order to open a file for writing to a text file is:

ofstream textfile("thefile.txt");

To open a file for reading a text file:

ifstream textfile("thefile.txt");

Closing a text file

When we have finished either writing or reading a text file, we need to close it so it does not keep using up the operating systems memory. This is achieved by:

textfile.close();

Binary files Input/Output

While handling text files is easy, it is always not the most efficient way to handle files. There will be times when you need to store unsorted binary data which is not text. To read and write blocks of binary data, the following prototypes are:

ofstream(memory_block, size);

ifstream(memory_block, size);

The code sample of binary files is a program dealing with an array with values, which creates a binary file and opens it. After it has been created, a block of data is written then the array is cleared. When the array is cleared,

58

the file which has just been created is now loaded in and read into the program. The values written from the binary file are then displayed in the output of the program.

```
/*

  Reading and writing a block of binary data

*/


#include <iostream>
#include <fstream>
#include <string>

using namespace std;

int main()
{
        int block[5] = {5, 4, 3, 2, 1};
        register int i;

        // Write the text file
        ofstream out("textfile", ios::binary);

        if(!out)
        {
                cout << "Cannot open the file\n";
                return 1;
        }

        // Write the block of data
        out.write((char *) &block, sizeof block);

        out.close();

        // Clear the array
        for(int i = 0; i < 5; i++)
                block[i] = 0;

        // Read the file
        ifstream in("textfile", ios::binary);
```

```cpp
    // If the file cannot be read
    if(!in)
    {
            cout << "Cannot open file\n";
            return 1;
    }

    // Read a block of data
    in.read((char *) &block, sizeof block);

    // Show the values read from the
    for(int i = 0; i < 5; i++)
    {
            cout << block[i] << " ";
    }

    in.close();

    return 0;
}
```

Value of the binary file output

```
5 4 3 2 1 Press any key to continue . . .
```

Structures

Structures originally came from the C language and are declared using the keyword "struct". In C++ the same principle applies as a group of data elements are grouped together under one name. Structures are very similar to classes but all the variables in a structure can be accessed. You will learn more about classes later in this book.

The variables in a structure are known as elements, and the elements can have different variable types and different lengths. An example of a struct is:

```
struct groceries
{
    // members of the struct
    string name;
    int weight;
    double price;

} chips, drinks;       // Objects of the structure
```

Once the members of the struct are defined, you can access the members directly by using a "." between the object name and the member name.

chips.name = "Smith Chips";

chips.weight = 500;

chips.price = 3.00;

drinks.name = "Coke";

drinks.weight = 500;

drinks.price = 2.50;

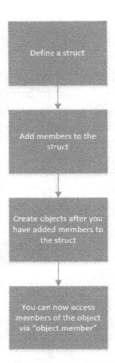

In the code sample of structures, we are continuing on with the example of defining a struct. In the body of the code, the objects and members are being set values and are then outputted on the program.

```
/*
 Structures example
 */

#include <iostream>
#include <fstream>
#include <string>

using namespace std;

struct groceries
{
        // members of the struct
        string name;
        int weight;
        double price;
```

```cpp
} chips, drinks;    // Objects of the structure

int main()
{
        // Set data for members of the struct
        chips.name = "Smith Chips";
        chips.weight = 500;
        chips.price = 3.00;

        drinks.name = "Coke";
        drinks.weight = 500;
        drinks.price = 2.50;

        // Output the values of the members
        cout << chips.name << "\n";
        cout << chips.weight << "\n";
        cout << chips.price << "\n" << "\n";

        cout << drinks.name << "\n";
        cout << drinks.weight << "\n";
        cout << drinks.price << "\n";

        return 0;
}
```

Output of the example struct code

63

Functions

Without functions in C++, the program will not run. The function we have been using in the code examples is "int main()". In this chapter we are going to be looking at writing our own functions. Functions are the building blocks of a C++ program. In fact, normal computer applications written in C++ will have hundreds of functions.

The general form of a function is:

```
variable_type variable_name(parameter_list)
{
    // Body of the function
}
```

Understanding what is going on here might be hard to understand at first but with the sample code, we will go through what is happening step by step.

Creating Functions

The variable types you can use when you are creating your own functions are exactly the same variable types you use to declare identifiers such as int, double, void and long. The steps to create a functions follows:

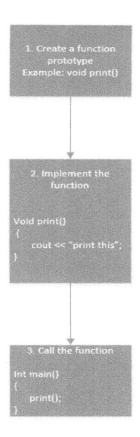

1. Create a function prototype
Example: void print()

2. Implement the function

Void print()
{
    cout << "print this";
}

3. Call the function

Int main()
{
    print();
}

What is void?

Void is something we haven't come across yet in this book. The definition of void in C++ is that it means nothing so when you are using the void keyword, it will not return a value. In the sample code we will declare two of our own functions.

```
1  /*
2       Creating Functions example
3     */
4
5    #include <iostream>
6
7    using namespace std;
8
9    // This is the function prototypes
10   void box_calculation(int length, int width, int height);
11   void display_title();
12
13   int main()
14   {
15       // Calling the display title function
16       display_title();
17
18       // Calling the box_calcualtion function
19       // This will now compute the volume
20       box_calculation(5, 4, 3);
21
22       return 0;
23   }

26   //---------------------------------------------
27   // Box calculation function implementation
28   //---------------------------------------------
29   void box_calculation(int length, int width, int height)
30   {
31       cout << "Volume of the box is " << length * width * height << "\n";
32   }
33
34
35   //---------------------------------------------
36   // Display name function implementation
37   //---------------------------------------------
38   void display_title()
39   {
40       cout << "Volume of a box calculator\n";
41   }
```

Understanding this code

Lines 10 - 11: In these lines we are declaring the **function prototypes**. Without declaring the function prototypes, the compiler will not run the code and will generate a complicated error that is impossible to understand.

As you can see with the declaration of void box_calculation(int length, int width, int height)

66

there are int values in the brackets. These are known as parameters of the function. These int values will be used to calculate the volume of the box.

```
void box_calculation(int length, int width, int height)



        // Calling the box_calcualtion function
        // This will now compute the volume
        box_calculation(5, 4, 3);
```

Other values you can pass in function parameters are pointers, arrays and strings, not just int and double variables.

Line 16: This is calling the display_title(); function which will execute the body code of the display_title function that was implemented under the int main() code in lines 38 - 40.

```
//----------------------------------------------
// Display name function implementation
//----------------------------------------------
void display_title()
{
        cout << "Volume of a box calculator\n";
}
```

Line 26 - 32: This is implementing the box calculation function prototype. Without implementing the function prototype, the calculation is not possible.

```
//----------------------------------------------
// Box calculation function implementation
//----------------------------------------------
void box_calculation(int length, int width, int height)
{
        cout << "Volume of the box is " << length * width * height << "\n";
}
```

Visual flowchart of the functions we have created in the sample code

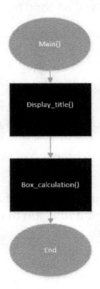

Returning functions

So far the only return value we have used in our sample codes in the book is "return 0". With the help of creating our own functions, we can use the return keyword to return values our functions have generated.

When you are returning values, you cannot use the void keyword, as void does not support returning values.

```cpp
1   /*
2       Returning Functions example
3   */
4
5   #include <iostream>
6
7   using namespace std;
8
9   // This is the function prototypes
10  double box_calculation(double length, double width, double height);
11
12  int main()
13  {
14      double answer;
15
16      // Calling the box_calcualtion function
17      // This will now compute the volume
18      answer = box_calculation(5.5, 4.3, 3.8);
19
20      // Display value
21      cout << "The volume is " << answer << "\n";
22
23      return 0;
24  }
25
26  //-----------------------------------------------
27  // Box calculation function implementation
28  //-----------------------------------------------
29  double box_calculation(double length, double width, double height)
30  {
31      return length * width * height;
32  }
33
```

69

Visual Diagram of understanding the return keyword from the sample code

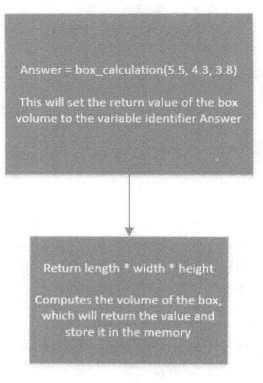

Answer = box_calculation(5.5, 4.3, 3.8)

This will set the return value of the box volume to the variable identifier Answer

Return length * width * height

Computes the volume of the box, which will return the value and store it in the memory

Function overloading

In C++, there a concept called function overloading where you define a function of the same name as long as the function parameter declarations are different. Let's look at a simple example:

```
/*
 Returning Functions example
 */

#include <iostream>

using namespace std;

// Function prototype declarations
void calculation(int i);
void calculation(double i, double j);
void calculation(double i, double j, double k);
```

```cpp
int main()
{
        // Call the functions
        calculation(10);

        calculation(10.50, 20.50);

        calculation(10.50, 20.50, 30.50);
        return 0;
}


//-------------------------------------------------
// Function implementations
//-------------------------------------------------
void calculation(int i )
{
        cout << "Function 1\n";
        cout << i << "\n\n";
}

void calculation(double i, double j)
{
        cout << "Function 2\n";
    cout << i * j << "\n\n";
}

void calculation(double i, double j, double k)
{
        cout << "Function 3\n";
        cout << i * j * k << "\n";
}
```

71

Sample output of the three overloading functions

```
Function 1
10

Function 2
215.25

Function 3
6565.13
Press any key to continue . . .
```

Classes

Up until now, you have been coding programs that have not used any of C++ object- orientated capabilities. To write object-orientated programs, you will need to use classes. Classes are just like the *structs* that we covered in a previous chapter, where they contain data members but they can also contain functions as members.

The general form of a class

```
class class_name
{
        private_data;
        private_functions;

    public:
        public_data;
        public_functions;
}; object_names;
```

The advantage of using classes instead of structs is that we can set the data to be either public, protected or private. By default all data and functions are private when declared in a class. By using classes all the variables and functions declared are encapsulated, which means they are all put together into a single unit as shown with the diagram below.

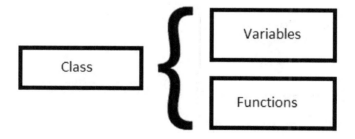

What is the difference between public, private and protected?

Public members can be accessed anywhere if the object is able to be found

Private members, no one other than the own class can access the members

Protected members can only be accessed by its own class and its shared members (shared members will be taught in a later chapter called inheritance).

Example of a defined class

```
//----------------------------------------------------
// The car class
//----------------------------------------------------
class Car
{
public:
        // Members of the car class
        int passengers;
        int fuel_capacity;

        string engine;
};
```

Basic class implementation of the car class

```
/*
Simple class example
*/

#include <iostream>
#include <string>

using namespace std;

//-----------------------------------------------
// The car class
//-----------------------------------------------
class Car
{
public:
        // Members of the car class
        int passengers;
        int fuel_capacity;

        string engine;
```

```cpp
};

int main()
{
        // Creating an object of the car class
        Car bmw;

        // Assign values from the Car class
        bmw.passengers = 5;
        bmw.fuel_capacity = 60;
        bmw.engine = "V8";

        // Display the set values
        cout << "passengers " << bmw.passengers << "\n";
        cout << "Fuel capacity " << bmw.fuel_capacity << "\n";
        cout << "Engine " << bmw.engine << "\n";
}
```

Output of the car class

```
passengers 5
Fuel capacity 60
Engine V8
Press any key to continue . . .
```

Adding in functions to a class

So far the example car class only contains data, but no functions. We can easily add in a function by entering a function prototype.

```
//-------------------------------------------------------
// The car class
//-------------------------------------------------------
class Car
{
public:
    // Members of the car class
    int passengers;
    int fuel_capacity;

    string engine;

    // Functions of the car class
    int car_weight();
};
```

Implementing a function from a class

When you are implementing a function from a class, you must tell the compiler what type of function it is. For example the int consuption() is set up by

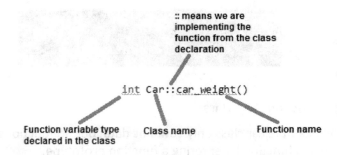

:: means we are implementing the function from the class declaration

int Car::car_weight()

Function variable type declared in the class

Class name

Function name

As you can see the :: operator we are implementing a function from a class. This links a class name with a member name in order to tell the compiler what class the member belongs to. In this example the "car_weight()" belongs to the Car class.

```
//----------------------------------------
// Car Weight implementation
//----------------------------------------
int Car::car_weight()
{
    int total;
    int carweight = 2000;

    return total = passengers * carweight;
}
```

Constructors and Destructors

Constructors and Destructors is a common concept in object-orientated programming. The definition of a constructor is that they are used to initialize an object when it is created. When you use a constructor, you will give initial values to variables defined in the class.

The Destructor does the opposite of a constructor. When objects in a class are no longer being used, the destructor can de-allocate memory it previously took up.

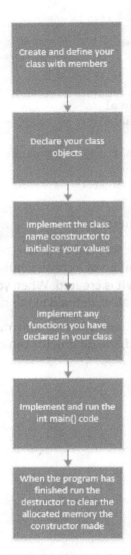

In the car class example, we initialized our values in the int main() code. This code example is a constructor initializing the set values.

```
/*
Constructor example
*/

#include <iostream>
#include <string>
```

```cpp
using namespace std;

//------------------------------------------------
// The car class
//------------------------------------------------
class Car
{
public:
        // Members of the car class
        int passengers;
        int fuel_capacity;

        string engine;

        // Functions of the car class
        int car_weight();

        // Create car constructor function
        Car();
};

//------------------------------------------------
// Car constructor implementation
//------------------------------------------------
Car::Car()
{
        passengers = 5;
        fuel_capacity = 60;
        engine = "V8";

}

//------------------------------------------------
// Car Weight implementation
//------------------------------------------------
int Car::car_weight()
{
        int total;
        int carweight = 2000;

        return total = passengers * carweight;
```

```
}

int main()
{
        // Creating an object of the car class
        Car bmw;

        // Display the set values
        cout << "passengers " << bmw.passengers << "\n";
        cout << "Fuel capacity " << bmw.fuel_capacity << "\n";
        cout << "Engine " << bmw.engine << "\n";

        // Display car weight
        cout << "Car Weight " << bmw.car_weight() << "\n";
}
```

Output of the set values of the constructor

```
passengers 5
Fuel capacity 60
Engine U8
Car Weight 10000
Press any key to continue . . .
```

Adding in a destructor to the Car class

To add in a destructor to the class, all you have to do is add in a "~" next to the name of the class name.

```
        // Create constructor function
        Car();

        // Deconstructor function
        ~Car();
```

When you are implementing a destructor in the code, you do not need to manually configure each variable in the class as the compiler will automatically do it.

```
// -------------------------------------------------
// Car deconstructor implementation
// -------------------------------------------------
Car::~Car()
{
    cout << "Deconstructing values\n";
}
```

```
passengers 5
Fuel capacity 60
Engine U8
Car Weight 10000

Deconstructing values
Press any key to continue . . .
```

As soon as the values of the class have been displayed, the destructor will then clear the allocated memory of the variables.

Overloading constructors

Just like how functions can be overloaded with different version of parameters, C++ also supports the same thing with constructors. The compiler will automatically be able to recall which parameters match when it is compiling the code.

Overloading Constructors with different parameters

Area() – Default constructor will be called as the parameters are empty

Area(int, int) – The default constructor will not be called

81

```
/*
Overloading class constructors
*/

#include <iostream>

using namespace std;

//----------------------------------------
// Area class declaration
//----------------------------------------
class Area
{
        int width, height;

public:
        Area();         // Default constructor
        Area(int, int);    // Overloading constructor with variables in
parameters

        int total_area();  // Total area function
};

//----------------------------------------
/// Default constructor implementation
//----------------------------------------
Area::Area()
{
        width = 10;
        height = 10;
}

//----------------------------------------
// Overloading constructor implementation
//----------------------------------------
Area::Area(int i, int j)
{
        width = i;
        height = j;
```

```
        }

//-----------------------------------------
// Total area function implementation
//-----------------------------------------
int Area::total_area()
{
        return width * height;
}

int main()
{
        Area rect1(3,4);        // Overloading constructor Area(int i, int j)
        Area rectb;             // Default constructor Area()

        // Display total area of rectangles
        cout << "Area of rectangle 1" << rect1.total_area() << "\n";
        cout << "Area of rectangle 2" << rectb.total_area() << "\n";

        return 0;
}
```

Headers

An helpful thing to know when programming classes in C++ is that you don't have to put all of your code in the same file. There is a file you can add in called headers where you can store your class definitions in a separate file. Follow these steps to create a header file:

Step 1: Right click on the header files folder, click add and choose new item

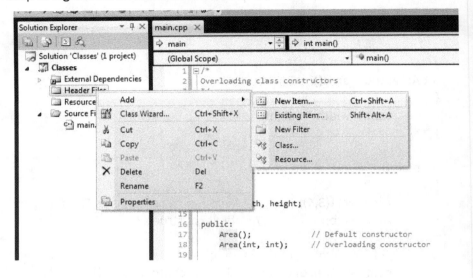

Step 2: Chose the "Header File(.h)" option and give it a name

Step 3: Copy or rewrite the class definition into the header file

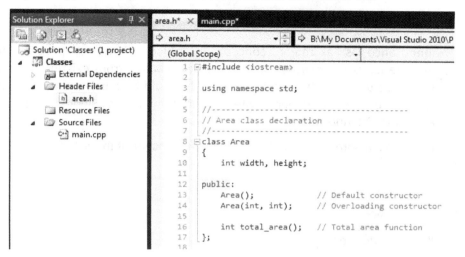

```
1   #include <iostream>
2
3   using namespace std;
4
5   //---------------------------------------------
6   // Area class declaration
7   //---------------------------------------------
8   class Area
9   {
10      int width, height;
11
12  public:
13      Area();                  // Default constructor
14      Area(int, int);          // Overloading constructor
15
16      int total_area();        // Total area function
17  };
18
```

Step 4: Go to the source files and double click on the main.cpp or whatever you named it and delete the class declaration code as it has all been declared in the header file now. Delete also the #include <iostream> and using namespace std as that is now included in the header file.

Step 5: Now we have to include the header file we just created otherwise the program will not run. Just like you would normally type in #include <iostream>, type in the name of the header file you created just like the following example

```
#include "area.h"
```

Step 6: Now you are now utilizing C++ object-orientated features. Give yourself a pat on the back for getting the hang of it.

Inheritance

Inheritance is a major concept in object-orientated programming. Inheritance is the process of forming new classes from existing classes. If you were to create two similar classes, it would be much more efficient to share the same members instead recreating of new ones. This is the advantage of inheritance.

Let's look at some code that applies to the concept of inheritance.

```
/*
Inheritance Example
*/

#include <iostream>

using namespace std;

//---------------------------------------------
// Shape class declaration
//---------------------------------------------
class Shape
{
protected:

        // Protected members can be accessed with the
        // help of inheritance
        int width, height;

public:
        void set_shape_values (int a, int b);
};


//---------------------------------------------
// Triangle class declaration
// This class will inherit the members of the
// Shape class
//---------------------------------------------
class Triangle : public Shape
{
```

```cpp
public:
        int Triangle_area_cal();
};

//-------------------------------------------------
// Rectangle class declaration
// This class will inherite the members of the
// shape class
//-------------------------------------------------
class Rectangle : public Shape
{
public:
        int Rectangle_area_cal();
};

//-------------------------------------------------
// Set shape function implementation
//-------------------------------------------------
void Shape::set_shape_values(int a, int b)
{
    // Set the values from the parameters
        width = a;
        height = b;
}

//-------------------------------------------------
// Triangle_area_cal function implementation
//-------------------------------------------------
int Triangle::Triangle_area_cal()
{
        return width * height / 2;
}

//-------------------------------------------------
// Rectangle_area_cal function implementation
//-------------------------------------------------
int Rectangle::Rectangle_area_cal()
{
        return width * height;
}
```

```cpp
int main()
{
        // Create the objects
        Triangle trig1;
        Rectangle rect1;

        // Set values
        trig1.set_shape_values(5, 5);
        rect1.set_shape_values(3, 5);

        // Display values
        cout << trig1.Triangle_area_cal() << "\n";
        cout << rect1.Rectangle_area_cal() << "\n";

        return 0;
}
```

Output of the inheritance code example

```
Triangle Area is 12
Rectangle Area is 15
Press any key to continue . . .
```

To explain how inheritance is working in this code example, have a look at the visual diagram.

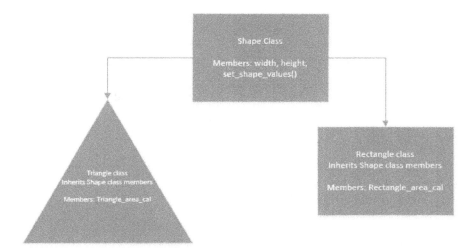

Firstly we have defined the first class named Shape. The members are width, height and set_shape_values(). Now when the triangle class and rectangle class are being declared, the way the shape class members are being inherited is by:

class **Triangle** : public **Shape**

class **Rectangle** : public **Shape**

Once the class declaration are completed, the functions in the three classes are then implemented

```
//---------------------------------------------
// Set shape function implementation
//---------------------------------------------
void Shape::set_shape_values(int a, int b)
{
    // Set the values from the parameters
        width = a;
        height = b;
}

//---------------------------------------------
// Triangle_area_cal function implementation
//---------------------------------------------
```

```cpp
int Triangle::Triangle_area_cal()
{
    // Formula for area of a triangle
        return width * height / 2;
}


//-----------------------------------------------
// Rectangle_area_cal function implementation
//-----------------------------------------------
int Rectangle::Rectangle_area_cal()
{
    // Formula for area of a rectangle
        return width * height;
}
```

After all the member functions have been implemented, we can now enter in the int main() code where we create two class objects and enter in values to calculate the area of the rectangle and triangle:

```cpp
// Create the objects
Triangle trig1;
Rectangle rect1;


// Set values
trig1.set_shape_values(5, 5);
rect1.set_shape_values(3, 5);
```

Once this has been done, we can then display the calculated values:

```cpp
// Display values
cout << trig1.Triangle_area_cal() << "\n";
cout << rect1.Rectangle_area_cal() << "\n";
```

Table summary of how we can access members via inheritance

	Public	Private	Protected

Members of the same class	Yes	Yes	Yes
Members of an inherited class	Yes	No	Yes
Not members	Yes	No	No

In the Shape class code, there are two protected members, width and height. These protected members can be accessed because the Rectangle and Triangle class inherit the Shape class members. If width and height were private members, they would only be able to be accessed under the same class name.

Multiple inheritance

When you are creating new classes, you can inherit more than one class at a time when needed. The way to inherit more than one class is to just separate the declaration with a comma. In this code example, we will go through code with a class containing multiple inherited classes

```cpp
#include <iostream>

using namespace std;

//---------------------------------------------
// Car class definition
//---------------------------------------------
class Car
{
protected:
        string fuel_type_car;

public:
        void display_car_fuel_type();
};

//---------------------------------------------
// Motorbike class definition
//---------------------------------------------
class MotoBike
{
protected:
```

```cpp
        string fuel_type_motobike;

public:
        void display_motobike_fuel_type();
};


//----------------------------------------------
// Vehicle class definition
// Inheriting the Car and Motorbike members
//----------------------------------------------
class Vehicles: public Car, public MotoBike
{
public:
        void show_values(string a, string b);
};


//----------------------------------------------------
// Display car fuel type function implementation
//----------------------------------------------------
void Car::display_car_fuel_type()
{
        cout << "Unleaded Fuel\n";
}


//----------------------------------------------------
// Display Motorbike fuel type implementation
//----------------------------------------------------
void MotoBike::display_motobike_fuel_type()
{
        cout << "Diesel fuel \n";
}


//----------------------------------------------------
// Show values of Vehicle class implementation
//----------------------------------------------------
void Vehicles::show_values(string a, string b)
{
    // Set parameter variables to class member variables
        a = fuel_type_car;
        b = fuel_type_motobike;
```

```
}

int main()
{
        // Create an object
        Vehicles v1;

        // Display fuel types with the help
        // of multiple inheritance
        v1.display_car_fuel_type();
        v1.display_motobike_fuel_type();
}
```

Output of multiple inheritance code

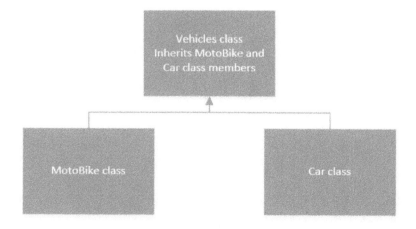

Visual Diagram of the multiple inheritance code

The multiple inheritance code example is very similar to the first code example of inheritance. It's only the Vehicle class code that is different because it is inheriting more than one class by "public Car, public MotoBike", as you can see below in the example.

```
//----------------------------------------------
// Vehicle class definition
// Inheriting the Car and Motorbike members
//----------------------------------------------
class Vehicles: public Car, public MotoBike
{
public:
          void show_values(string a, string b);
};
```

Virtual functions and polymorphism

This is going to be a tricky chapter as virtual functions and polymorphism are the most complicated concepts in C++ object-orientated programming. A virtual function is simply a function that is declared **virtual** in a base class and overridden in a derived class.

The reason why virtual functions are used is because they support polymorphism. Polymorphism is the ability to process objects differently depending on their data type or class. Just like inheritance, polymorphism enables the programmer to define different methods for any number of derived classes. Polymorphism is also applied to function overloading, as shown in the chapter explaining functions, where we showcase multiple functions with the same name but containing different items in the parameters.

A great real-life example of polymorphism would be a start-up entrepreneur. The person who starts a company by him/herself will have to wear different hats to bring the company to life doing the sales, marketing, customer service and hiring of employees. The person is still the same but is conducting different jobs within the same company.

An example of declaring a virtual function is:

```
virtual void virtual_base();
```

Once the virtual function has been defined in a class, it will need to be redefined in other class declarations except without the "virtual" keyword.

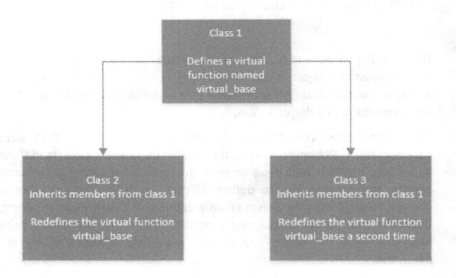

The code sample below puts this visual diagram into practice by defining three classes named Base, Output_one and Output_two. The classes Output_one and Output_two apply the concept of inheritance to set up the declaration of the virtual function declared in the Base class.

```
/*
Inheritance example
*/

#include <iostream>

using namespace std;


//-------------------------------------------------
// Base Virtual class declaration
//-------------------------------------------------
class Base
{
public:
        // This is a virtual function
        virtual void virtual_base();
};
```

96

```
//-----------------------------------------------
// Class output one declaration
//-----------------------------------------------
class Output_one : public Base
{
public:
        // This will redefine the virtual function for the
        // Output_one class
        void virtual_base();
};


//-----------------------------------------------
// Class output two declaration
//-----------------------------------------------
class Output_two : public Base
{
public:
        // This will redefine the virtual function a second
    // time for the Output two class
        void virtual_base();
};


//-----------------------------------------------
// Implementing the functions from the classes
//-----------------------------------------------
void Base::virtual_base()
{
        cout << "This will output the virtual function\n\n";
}


void Output_one::virtual_base()
{
        cout << "This will output the defined virtual function for Output
1\n\n";
}
void Output_two::virtual_base()
{
        cout << "This will output the defined virtual function for Output
2\n\n";
}
```

```cpp
int main()
{

        // Create Base class object
        Base base_object;

        // Create Output_one and Output_two object
        Output_one output_one_object;
        Output_two output_two_object;

        // Assign deference pointer
        Base *p;

        // Return memory address
        p = &base_object;

        // Call the virtual function through a base class pointer
        p->virtual_base();

        // Return memory address
        p = &output_one_object;

        // Call the virtual function through a base class pointer
        p->virtual_base();

        // Return memory address
        p = &output_two_object;

        // Call the virtual function through a base class pointer
        p->virtual_base();

        return 0;
}
```

This sample code will produce the following output

```
This will output the virtual function
This will output the defined virtual function for Output 1
This will output the defined virtual function for Output 2
Press any key to continue . . .
```

Let's run through what is going on here. Firstly we are defining three classes. In the Base class we are defining our virtual function. This means we can redefine it in a derived class which is exactly what happens in the Output_one and Output_two classes. The Base class has been inherited and the virtual function has been redefined without the "virtual" keyword.

```
//------------------------------------------------
// Class output one declaration
//------------------------------------------------
class Output_one : public Base
{
public:
        // This will redefine the virtual function for the
        // Output_one class
        void virtual_base();
};


//------------------------------------------------
// Class output two declaration
//------------------------------------------------
class Output_two : public Base
{
public:
        // This will redefine the virtual function a second
    // time for the Output two class
        void virtual_base();
};
```

The function members inside the classes are then implemented with output text in each one, showcasing outputting the declared virtual function and derived virtual functions.

```
//-----------------------------------------------
// Implementing the functions from the classes
//-----------------------------------------------
void Base::virtual_base()
{
        cout << "This will output the virtual function\n\n";
}

void Output_one::virtual_base()
{
        cout << "This will output the defined virtual function for Output
1\n\n";
}

void Output_two::virtual_base()
{
        cout << "This will output the defined virtual function for Output
2\n\n";
}
```

Inside the int main(), we are applying pointers here along with creating the class objects base_object, output_one_object and output_two_object.

```
        // Create Base class object
        Base base_object;

        // Create Output_one and Output_two object
        Output_one output_one_object;
        Output_two output_two_object;

    // Assign deference pointer
        Base *p;
```

Since virtual_base() is declared as a virtual function, the compiler will determine which version of virutal_base() to execute based on the pointer "p". In the first case, p points to an object of the Base class, so the version of virtual_base() is executed in the program.

The next step shows that pointer p is assigned to the address of Output_one_object. The compiler will then check again what type of object the pointer p is pointing to and determines what version of virutal_base() to execute. The same step happens when the pointer p is assigned to the address of Output_two_object. The version of virtual_base() will be executed inside the Output_two_object class.

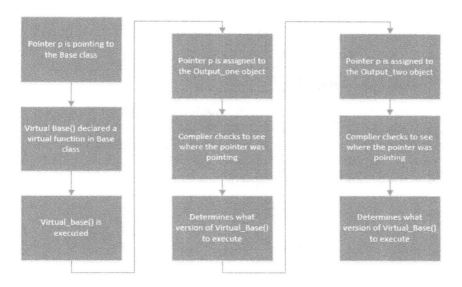

// Call the virtual function through a base class pointer
    p->virtual_base();

    // Return memory address
    p = &output_one_object;

    // Call the virtual function through a base class pointer
    p->virtual_base();

    // Return memory address
    p = &output_two_object;

    // Call the virtual function through a base class pointer
    p->virtual_base();

Remember when a virtual function is called through a base class pointer, the version of the virtual function actually executed is determined by the compiler and the type of object being pointed to.

Templates

What is a template?

A template is a sophisticated feature in the C++ language which allows programmers to create generic functions and classes. By being able to use templates to create generic functions and classes, this allows us to use different data types which can be reused again.

Function templates

A function template behaves like a normal C++ function but the advantage it has when a template is used is that it can support many different types of data. When the compiler is running the code, it will create a different version for the function when there are different types of data being used. The code example of Function templates will explain this clearly.

```
1  //-------------------------------------------------
2  // Function Template example
3  //-------------------------------------------------
4  #include <iostream>
5  #include <string>
6
7  using namespace std;
8  //-------------------------------------------------
9  // Creating the function template
10 // void swap_values() is a generic function that
11 // will swap the values
12 //-------------------------------------------------
13 template <class T> void swap_values(T &a, T&b)
14 {
15     // Creating a class object that will help swap the values
16     T TempSwitch;
17     TempSwitch = a;
18
19     a = b;
20     b = TempSwitch;
21 }
22
```

```
23  □int main()
24   {
25        // Original values to be shown
26        int i = 5, j = 20;
27        float x = 50.5, y = 60.2;
28        string name1 = "Sahil", name2 = "Tony";
29
30        cout << "Original values " << i << ", " << j << "\n";
31        cout << "Original values " << x << ", " << y << "\n";
32        cout << "Original values " << name1 << ", " << name2 << "\n\n";
33
34
35  □     // Calling the swapValues function from the Template which
36        // Will create a separate version for each swapValues data type
37        // In the parameters (brackets)
38        swap_values(i, j);
39        swap_values(x, y);
40        swap_values(name1, name2);
41
42        // Display the values that have now been swapped
43        cout << "Swapped values " << i << ", " << j << "\n";
44        cout << "Swapped values " << x << ", " << y << "\n";
45        cout << "Swapped values " << name1 << ", " << name2 << "\n";
46
47        return 0;
48   }
```

Class Templates

Class Templates allows programmers to create a normal class which defines all the components used by that class but the actual data being manipulated will be specified by what kind of data is inside the parameter (brackets) of the class. This can be useful when you are implementing a data structure like a linked list as an example. Normally you wouldn't need to implement a linked list by yourself as it is built in the C++ Standard Template Library. When you are using integers for a linked list, a class template will allow you to with any type of data. Let's look at some example code of a class template that is used for division program:

```
10    //-------------------------------------------------
11    // Creating the class template
12    //-------------------------------------------------
13    template <class I> class Calculation
14    {
15        // Create the class objects
16        I x, y;
17
18    public:
19        // Set the values in the parameters
20        // to the class objects declared
21        Calculation(I a, I b)
22        {
23            x = a;
24            y = b;
25        }
26
27        // Create a math function that will
28        // Divide the class objects x/y
29        I div()
30        {
31            return x / y;
32        }
33
34    };

37    int main()
38    {
39        // Create a version of class I for doubles
40        Calculation<float> f_ob(10,3);
41        cout << "float division: " << f_ob.div() << "\n";
42
43        // Create a version of class I for integers
44        Calculation<int> i_ob(10,3);
45        cout << "integer division: " << i_ob.div() << "\n";
46
47        return 0;
48    }
```

The most important concept to understand with templates

The main concept to understand with templates is that they can allow us to generate functions and classes which allow us to reuse different data types without being rewritten every time for each one.

Basics of C++ Template Metaprogramming

What is Template Metaprogramming?

We all know that when we are writing a program, we are coding a sequence of instructions which creates and modifies data. The simplest way to describe what Template metaprogramming does, is that metaprogramming is a sequence of instructions which modifies and creates programs. C++ templates that have been created can be customized at compile time with the help of metaprogramming.

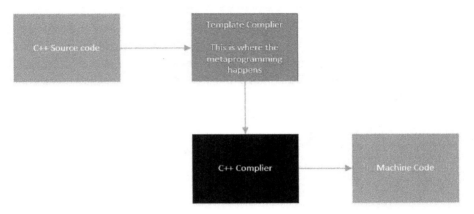

When we were introduced to C++ Templates, there were two major types of templates which were template functions and class templates. As the name says, a template function is not a function at all and the same goes for class templates. They are simply used as a template to **generate functions and classes**. What you just read sounds really confusing. Let's go down deeper with this concept. When you are using templates and you are running the code, it will generate different data types without being rewritten every time for each one as a template that will be reused.

An example would be the std::vector as it is actually not a class. It is a template built in the C++ Standard template library which applies C++ templates to generate the correct vector class for each type of data type being used. When std::vector<double> is used, the compiler will generate the code for a vector of doubles and vice versa if integers were used.

Metafunctions are the basic unit of metaprogramming. Meta functions is simply a function working with **types** which the entities can be manipulated.

Lets's look at an example of a simple metafunction

```
1   template<typename T>
2   struct throw_balls
3   {
4       using type = T;
5   };
6
7   template<typename T>
8   struct throw_balls<T*>
9   {
10      using type = typename throw_balls<T>::type;
11  };
```

In line 10, the template throw_balls is the metafunction which takes a type and throws away all the balls. The key concept to take away from this example is metaprogramming is used to generate code automatically. This is only a very brief example of template metaprogramming as they go deeper into design patterns, code optimization and many other advanced programming topics.

Namespaces

When you were first starting to learn the C++ language, you might of noticed a common line which was "**using namespace std**" in all your basic applications. This is because the entire library is defined in its own namespace called std. By declaring std, it gives you direct access to the names of the functions and classes within the C++ library, without having to insert each one with **std::**.

As you eventually reach an advance level understanding C++, you may not want to declare the standard C++ library by inserting "using namespace std" if your code will only be using a small amount of the library otherwise it would cause name conflicts during compiling. But if your code has several references to library names, then it's beneficial to declare the **std library**.

Purpose of Namespaces

In simple terms, namespaces in C++ are used to organise code by localising the name of variables in order to avoid name collisions which is useful for large projects. An example would be if you had a program where you defined a class **Overflow** and a library used in your program contains a class called **Overflow** as well.

This would lead to problems in compiling as there is a conflict with the names because both names are stored in the global namespace. The compiler has no way of knowing which version of **Overflow** class are referring to within your code. If we were to create a separate namespace for each **Overflow** class, the program would have no conflicts with the name of the class.

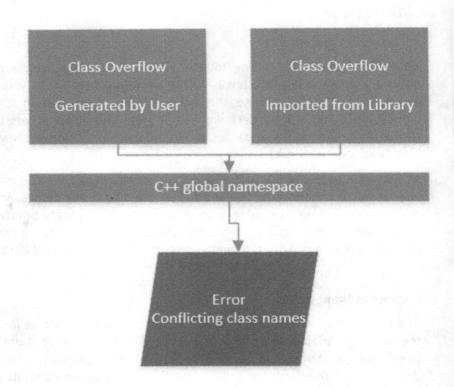

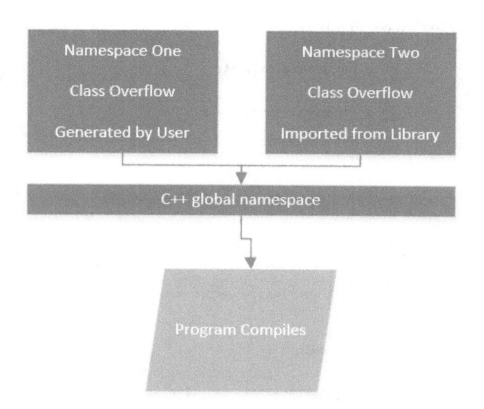

Creating your own namespace example code

```
1    #include <iostream>
2    using namespace std;
3
4    // first name space declaration
5    namespace first_space
6    {
7    void display_line()
8    {
9    cout << "Inside first namespace" << endl;
10   }
11   }
12
13   // second name space declaration
14   namespace second_space
15   {
16   void display_line()
17   {
18   cout << "Inside second namespace" << endl;
19   }
20   }
21
22   int main() {
23
24   // Calls function from first name space.
25   first_space::display_line();
26
27   // Calls function from second name space.
28   second_space::display_line();
29
30   return 0;
31   }
```

About the author

Sahil Bora is an embedded software engineer from Melbourne, Australia. He is the founder and proprietor of C++ Better Explained and also the author of the book How to Win at Mathematics. Since 2014, he has worked in multiple industries as an embedded software engineer including automotive electronics, IoT (Internet of Things) and academia.

He graduated from RMIT University Melbourne in 2017 with a degree in electrical/electronic engineering with honours. In his spare time, he enjoys going surfing and travelling. At the moment Sahil's current project is working on inventing and developing a wearable medical device to be out onto the market.

More information about Sahil Bora and the projects he's worked on can be found at http://sahilbora.com

www.ingramcontent.com/pod-product-compliance
Lightning Source LLC
Chambersburg PA
CBHW071226050326
40689CB00011B/2470